How to Draw the Life and Times of
Rutherford B. Hayes

Melody S. Mis

23ʀᴅ REGT OHIO VOLUNTEERS

The Rosen Publishing Group's
PowerKids Press™
New York

To my godchildren, who bring me great joy

Published in 2006 by The Rosen Publishing Group, Inc.
29 East 21st Street, New York, NY 10010

First Edition

Editor: Jennifer Way
Layout Design: Ginny Chu

Illustration Credits: Cover and interior illustrations by Jeffrey Wendt; p. 20 by Michelle Innes.
Photo Credits: P. 4 Courtesy of the Rutherford B. Hayes Presidential Center; pp. 7, 12, 16, 28 Library of Congress Prints and Photographs Division; pp. 8, 9, 18 Donald L. Mark; p. 10 Picture History; p. 14 Ohio Historical Society; p. 20 © Hulton-Deutsch Collection/Corbis; p. 22 Scott Dolson; p. 24 Thomas Nast illustration from *Harper's Weekly*; p. 26 Express Locomotive illustration from *The Railroad Gazette*.

Library of Congress Cataloging-in-Publication Data

Mis, Melody S.
  How to draw the life and times of Rutherford B. Hayes / Melody S. Mis.— 1st ed.
      p. cm. — (A kid's guide to drawing the presidents of the United States of America)
  Includes bibliographical references and index.
  ISBN 1-4042-2996-5 (lib. bdg. : alk. paper)
  1. Hayes, Rutherford Birchard, 1822–1893—Juvenile literature. 2. Presidents—United States—Biography—Juvenile literature. 3. Drawing—Technique—Juvenile literature. I. Title. II. Series.

E682.M68 2006
743.4'3—dc22
                                        2004025423

Manufactured in the United States of America

Contents

Rutherford B. Hayes

Rutherford B. Hayes was a lawyer, a soldier, a governor, and a president. He was one of the most honest politicians of his day, yet he is remembered as the man who stole the 1876 presidential election.

Rutherford Birchard Hayes was born on October 4, 1822, in Delaware, Ohio. He was the fifth child born to Rutherford and Sophia Birchard Hayes. Hayes attended private schools, where he was a good student and an excellent speller. In 1838, at age 16, Hayes entered Kenyon College in Gambier, Ohio. He graduated from Kenyon in 1842, and went on to study law at Harvard Law School in Cambridge, Massachusetts. After graduation in 1845, Hayes opened a law office in Fremont, Ohio, where his uncle, Sardis Birchard, lived. In 1850, Hayes moved to Cincinnati, Ohio, where he continued his law practice. Hayes courted Lucy Ware Webb in Cincinnati, and they married in 1852.

When the Civil War began in 1861, Hayes joined the 23rd Regiment of Ohio Volunteers. In 1864, Hayes was nominated for the U.S. House of Representatives. He did not leave the war to campaign, but he won the election anyway. In 1876, Hayes was nominated by the Republican Party to run for president.

The 1876 presidential election turned out to be one of the most dishonest elections in American history. The race was settled with a compromise between Democrats and Republicans. It was because of the compromise that many Democrats felt Hayes stole the election to become the nineteenth president.

You will need the following supplies to draw the life and times of Rutherford B. Hayes:

✓ A sketch pad ✓ An eraser ✓ A pencil ✓ A ruler

These are some of the shapes and drawing terms you need to know:

Horizontal Line	——		Squiggly Line	
Oval			Trapezoid	
Rectangle			Triangle	
Shading			Vertical Line	
Slanted Line			Wavy Line	

The Nineteenth President

When Rutherford B. Hayes took office on March 5, 1877, he promised to fulfill the conditions of the compromise made between the Democrats and the Republicans to bring him into office. These conditions included removing government troops from the southern states, which ended Reconstruction. He also agreed to appoint Democrats to government posts. At this time government jobs were given to friends and party members by what was called the spoils system. Although he agreed to do this, Hayes did not believe this system was fair. He believed that jobs should be given to the most qualified people.

Even though Hayes had to do these things to fulfill the election compromise, he accomplished many of his own goals. He reformed civil service and strengthened the office of the president. Because of his honesty, Hayes brought respectability back to the U.S. government. The government had been seen as dishonest during the two presidencies before Hayes's, those of Andrew Johnson and Ulysses S. Grant.

This photograph shows Rutherford B. Hayes's inauguration on March 5, 1877. The agreement between the Republicans and the Democrats, which gave the election to Hayes, had been reached only a few days before.

Hayes's Ohio

The Rutherford B. Hayes Presidential Library and Museum is in Fremont, Ohio. It has more than 13,000 objects that belonged to Hayes.

Map of the United States of America

In 1910, Rutherford and Lucy's son, Webb Hayes, gave the family home at Spiegel Grove to the state of Ohio, so that it could be preserved as a legacy to his father. Ohio honored the ex-president by building the Rutherford B. Hayes Presidential Library on the grounds at Spiegel Grove. Located in Fremont, Ohio, it is America's first presidential library. The library was built between 1912 and 1916. It has objects from Hayes's life, including his personal diaries, things from his Civil War service, and 12,000 of his books. The library was constructed of gray sandstone in the classical style of architecture, which features columns such as those found on ancient Greek buildings.

After Hayes died on January 17, 1893, he was buried at Oakwood Cemetery in Fremont. Lucy, who had died in 1889, had been buried there, too. In 1915, Hayes and Lucy were moved to a tomb, or grave, at Spiegel Grove. Part of Hayes's tomb was made from granite that came from a quarry near his father's farm in Vermont. The Hayes' tomb is now part of the Rutherford B. Hayes Presidential Center.

Rutherford B. Hayes and Lucy Webb Hayes are buried at Spiegel Grove. This is the marker for the grave.

Hayes's Birthplace

Rutherford B. Hayes was born in Delaware, Ohio, on October 4, 1822. His parents, Rutherford and Sophia Hayes, were

descendants of Scottish and English immigrants who had settled in Vermont. In 1817, the Hayes family moved from Vermont to a farm in Ohio.

Hayes was named after his father, who died before his son was born. After her husband's death, Sophia and her brother, Sardis Birchard, raised young Rutherford. They called him Ruddy. Because Hayes was often sick as a child, Sophia would not let him go to school until he was seven years old. Hayes then went on to study at private schools and enrolled at Kenyon College at age 16. After graduating from Kenyon in 1842, Hayes studied law at Harvard Law School. In 1845, he moved to Fremont, Ohio. Although Hayes's birthplace home, shown above, in Delaware, Ohio, no longer exists, there is a bronze marker located where the house once stood.

1

You will be drawing the front part of Rutherford B. Hayes's birthplace. To begin use a ruler to draw a rectangle. This will be your guide.

2

Draw a slanted shape inside your guide. This will be the front of the house.

3

Draw the roof of the house using a slanted shape. It looks like a rectangle that has been tipped to the left.

4

Draw the side of the house using five lines. Notice how the roof lines and the bottom lines are slanted.

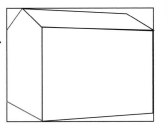

5

Erase the guide. Draw the window shapes on the front and the side of the house using rectangles. Draw a long, thin rectangle above the lower windows on the front.

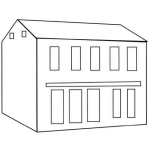

6

Add the window frames of the windows on the front of the house.

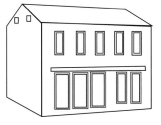

7

Make windowpanes on the front windows and the front door by drawing vertical and horizontal lines.

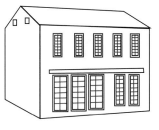

8

Shade your drawing of the house. Use darker shading to make the roof's shingles. Shade some of the windows darker. Good job!

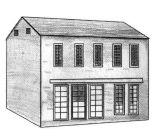

Meet Lucy Webb Hayes

Lucy Webb Hayes was born to James and Maria Cook Webb on August 28, 1831, in Chillicothe, Ohio. After Lucy's father died in 1833, her grandfather, Isaac Cook, helped raise her. Cook believed in temperance, which means he did not think people should drink alcohol. He encouraged Lucy to adopt the same belief.

In 1844, Lucy's family moved to Delaware, Ohio. She met Hayes there in 1847. That year Lucy enrolled at Wesleyan Female College in Cincinnati, Ohio. In 1850, Hayes moved to Cincinnati to practice law and began visiting Lucy at school. Two years later they married.

Once Hayes was elected president, Lucy became a popular First Lady. She would not allow alcohol to be served in the White House. This earned her the nickname "Lemonade Lucy." Lucy was the first president's wife to have graduated from college. Lucy died at Spiegel Grove on June 25, 1889.

1

Begin drawing Lucy Webb Hayes by making a guide oval for the head. Draw guidelines for the neck and body.

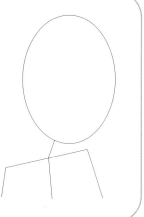

2

Draw guidelines on the front of the oval. These will help you position her facial features. Add an oval on the side of the head. This will become her ear. Draw a curved line on the head.

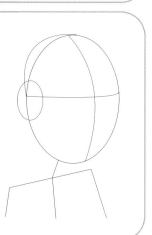

3

Draw the outline of the neck and shoulders. Draw a triangle as a guide for the nose. Draw almond-shaped ovals for eye guidelines. Draw a guideline for the mouth.

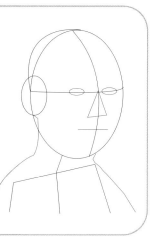

4

Draw the outline of her face and her ear using curved lines. Draw the outline of her hair using curved and wavy lines. Notice that her hair parts in the middle.

5

Erase the head and ear ovals. Draw the eyes and eyelids. Draw the nose. Draw the outline of the upper lip and the bottom curve of the lower lip.

6

Erase the guides for the eyes, the nose, and the mouth. Draw her dress and ruffled collar using many squiggly lines.

7

Erase the body outline and any extra lines. Draw the comb on top of her head. Add detail to the dress and collar using squiggly lines.

8

Finish with detail and shading. Parts of her hair are dark. Her dress is dark. The collar of the dress is white with shadowed lines.

Hayes and the Civil War

When the Civil War began in 1861, Rutherford B. Hayes was one of the first men to join the 23rd Regiment of Ohio Volunteers. The Ohio Volunteers' flag is shown here. The Civil War, which lasted from 1861 to 1865, was a war between the Southern

states and the Northern states. The Southern states had seceded from the Union. During his four years fighting for the Union in the Ohio Volunteers, Hayes rose to the rank of major general.

Hayes was shot in his left arm at the Battle of South Mountain on September 14, 1862. In November, after his arm had healed, Hayes rejoined the Ohio Volunteers. He continued to fight until the war ended.

In 1864, the Republican Party nominated Hayes as their candidate for the U.S. House of Representatives. He would not leave the war to campaign. He won the election despite this.

1

You will be drawing the flag of the 23rd Ohio Volunteers. To begin use a ruler to draw a rectangle.

2

Use a ruler to draw a rectangle in the upper left corner of the rectangle you drew in step 1.

3

Use the ruler to draw 12 horizontal lines inside the rectangle. Print the words, "23rd REGT OHIO VOLUNTEERS" on the seventh line down.

4

Using a ruler draw a border around the outside of the square. Draw the flagpole. On the top of the pole, draw an oval and make the guide shapes for the eagle.

5

Draw small stars inside the rectangle in the corner. Draw one star in each corner and one in the middle. Draw 10 stars around the center star. Draw 20 stars around the 10 stars. Draw short lines to fill the border on the top, right, and bottom. Draw the eagle.

6

Erase extra lines. Finish with shading. Use a pencil to shade in every other stripe of the flag. Press the pencil harder to shade in the corner rectangle around the stars. Good job!

The Governor of Ohio

In 1867, Rutherford B. Hayes left his post as a U.S. representative when he was elected governor of Ohio. He held this post from 1868 to 1872. He

was so popular that he was elected governor again in 1875. Hayes served his terms as governor in the Ohio Statehouse in Columbus, shown above.

Hayes was a successful governor. While Hayes was in office, he lowered the state's debt and worked to improve conditions in the state's hospitals, prisons, and schools. Hayes's interest in education led him to become one of the founders of Ohio State University in 1870. He supported safety rules for people who worked in the coal mines and on the railroads. Although Hayes accomplished many things as governor, he considered his role in giving Ohio's approval of the Fifteenth Amendment to the U.S. Constitution his most important accomplishment. This amendment protected the African Americans' right to vote.

1

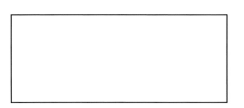

You will draw the Ohio Statehouse. To begin use a ruler to draw a rectangle.

2

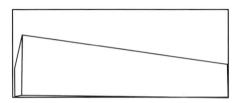

Draw the front and side of the building inside the guide rectangle using slanted lines.

3

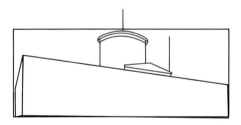

Draw a rotunda, the round shape on the building, using curved and straight lines. Add the shape in front of the rotunda using a triangle and straight lines. Draw two flagpoles.

4

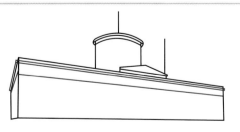

Erase the outer box. Use a ruler to draw lines on the upper part of the front and side of the building.

5

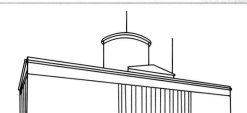

Use a ruler to draw the columns on the front and the side of the building.

6

Draw windows on the front of the building and on the rotunda using rectangles. Add detail to the rotunda. Add the triangle inside the triangle you added in step 3.

7

Add detail lines across the top of the building. Add a horizontal line along the upper part of the building.

8

Draw trees on the front lawn. Add detail and shading to the building. The windows and the spaces between the columns are the darkest.

Spiegel Grove

In 1873, Rutherford B. Hayes had completed his first two terms as Ohio's governor. He and his family then moved in with his uncle, Sardis Birchard,  at Spiegel Grove in Fremont, Ohio. Birchard had purchased the 25-acre (10 ha) estate in 1846.

Birchard built a two-story home on the property between 1859 and 1863. When Birchard died in 1874, he left Spiegel Grove to Hayes. During the years Hayes lived there, he made many additions to the home, including a library, a dining room, and a new kitchen. The dining room was designed to look like the one at the White House. Hayes loved trees and often named the ones on his property after people who visited him at Spiegel Grove. In 1877, Hayes had a reunion with the Ohio Volunteers, and he named five oak trees after some of his army friends. These trees are called the Reunion Oaks. Hayes also named trees after other important guests. Spiegel Grove was opened to the public in 1966.

1

You will be drawing Spiegel Grove. To begin use a ruler to draw a rectangle. This will be your guide in drawing the house.

2

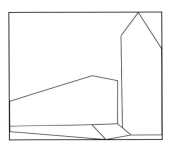

Draw the side of the house. Make the edge of the roof using slanted lines. Add the porch on the front of the house using slanted lines as shown.

3

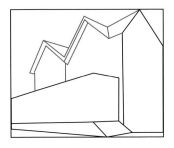

Draw the edges of the roof using slanted lines. Draw vertical lines on the front of the house.

4

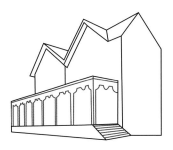

Erase the guide rectangle. Draw the pillars and decoration of the porch. Add stairs to the porch.

5

Draw windows on the front and side of the house. Draw shutters on the large front windows. Draw windowpanes on the front and side windows. Add windows and a door to the porch. Add chimneys to the roof.

6

Finish with detail and shading. Add a tree to the front yard. The areas under the porch and the windows are the darkest. Great job!

The Temperance Movement

Lucy and Rutherford Hayes did not believe in drinking alcohol. Hayes would not allow alcohol to be served at the White House, because he thought it was important to set a good example for others. Lucy was so against the use of alcohol that she joined the Women's Christian Temperance Union, which is called the WCTU.

The WCTU was founded in 1874 by a group of women in Cleveland, Ohio. Frances Willard, shown here, was president of the group from 1879 until 1898. They wanted to ban the sale and drinking of alcohol. The WCTU thought that the use of alcohol was hurting people's families. Their war against alcohol spread quickly. More than 250 towns in New York and Ohio banned alcohol within the first year after the WCTU was established. By the end of the nineteenth century, the WCTU had become the world's largest women's group.

1 Begin drawing Frances Willard with a rectangle. Draw an oval inside the rectangle. The oval is the guide for the head. Add a slanted line as a guide for the shoulders.

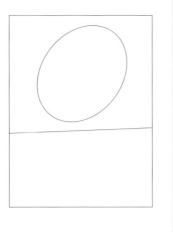

2 Next outline the shoulders of her dress. Then draw the outline of the front of her dress using squiggly lines.

3 Erase the slanted guideline. Finish the dress by adding lines to the shoulders. Add the ribbon pinned to the dress. This ribbon is the symbol of the WCTU.

4 Use the oval guide to outline the shape of the hair and face. Draw two straight lines in a cross form to use as guides for the facial features.

5 Erase the head oval. Now draw the face. Draw the shapes of the eyes and the eyebrows using curved lines. Add two ovals in front of the eyes for her glasses. Add the nose, the mouth, and the ear. Add the hairline.

6 Erase the face guide. Finish the drawing by adding detail shading. Notice that her dress is very dark. The WCTU ribbon can be left white.

The 1876 Election

In 1876, Rutherford B. Hayes was chosen as the Republican presidential candidate to run against the Democratic candidate, Samuel Tilden. The badge shown here is from Hayes's campaign.

When the election was over, Tilden had won the popular vote, which means he had the most votes. However, electoral votes, instead of the popular vote, decide who wins a presidential election. The popular vote tells who has won each state. Each state has a number of electoral votes based on its number of representatives. Neither candidate had enough electoral votes to win.

The two parties made a secret compromise. The Democrats would let Hayes win the election if he ended Reconstruction and appointed Democrats to important government positions. The Republicans agreed to the compromise without telling Hayes. On March 5, 1877, Hayes was sworn in as president.

1 You will be drawing one of Hayes's campaign badges from the 1876 election. To begin use a ruler to draw a rectangle. This will be your guide.

2 Inside your guide rectangle, draw a triangle. Draw three circles, one inside the other, as shown. The largest circle starts at the triangle's point and is in the left corner.

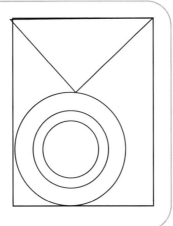

3 Erase the rectangle. Draw nine *V*'s inside the largest circle. Some are upside down or sideways. Draw an oval and three lines in the smallest circle. This will be a guide for Hayes's face and neck.

4 Draw the outline of Hayes's neck, shoulders, clothes, hair, and beard. Draw his eyes, nose, ear, and cheek.

5 Erase the face and neck guidelines. Inside the triangle draw the outline of the eagle.

6 Erase the triangle. Finish the outline of the eagle. Draw a shield on the eagle's chest. Using curved lines, connect the eagle to the badge.

7 Add details to the badge. Draw the eagle's feathers and face. Finish the shield on the eagle's chest. Draw lines to show the branches the eagle is holding in its feet. Finish Hayes's eyes, hair, and beard. Add lines around the badge. Finish with shading. Great job!

Ending Reconstruction

Rutherford B. Hayes honored the requirements of the 1876 election compromise soon after he took office as president in 1877. A month after his

inauguration, Hayes ended Reconstruction by removing all federal troops from southern states. Reconstruction was the name given to the time period following the Civil War. Among other things the plan said the southern states had to accept the three new amendments to the U.S. Constitution. These amendments banned slavery, granted citizenship to African Americans, and protected the African Americans' civil rights. The cartoon here shows the hope that these things would happen peacefully. In reality the struggle for civil rights would continue into the twentieth century. When Hayes ended Reconstruction, he had fulfilled one of the terms of the election compromise in good faith. He hoped to heal some of the anger left from the Civil War.

1

You will be drawing a political cartoon that represents the ending of Reconstruction. To begin use a ruler to draw a rectangle.

2

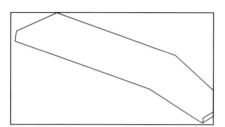

Using straight lines, draw the outline of the paper. Notice where the paper has a bend in it.

3

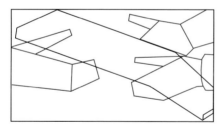

Draw the shapes of the three hands using straight lines. These will be guides for drawing the hands and wrists.

4

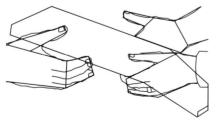

Erase the outer rectangle. Draw the outlines of the hands, fingers, and fingernails inside the hand guidelines. Draw the cuff and wrist of the hands on the right.

5

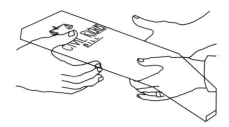

Erase the hand guidelines. On the paper write the words "CIVIL RIGHTS BILL." Draw a set of scales above the words. The scales represent justice.

6

Draw the ribbon around the middle of the bill. Erase the lines of the bill that go through the hands. Write the word "COLUMBIA" on the bracelet of the lower right hand. Columbia stands for the United States.

7

Use your pencil to shade the two hands on the right lightly. Shade shadows on the hands darkly. Shade the hand on the left darkly. Shade the ribbon darkly. Wonderful work!

The Great Railroad Strike

Reconstruction was not the only issue Rutherford B. Hayes had to deal with early in his presidency. In

1877, railroad workers in Pennsylvania, West Virginia, Maryland, and Illinois, went on strike in what became known as the Great Railroad Strike. The train shown here is similar to the trains in use at the time.

The railroad strike began in Pittsburgh, Pennsylvania, in July 1877. This was soon after the railroads had fired some of their workers and cut the salaries of the remaining workers in order to increase their companies' profits. When the Pittsburgh workers went on strike, coal miners, ironworkers, and steelworkers from nearby states joined the strike. Fighting soon broke out between the strikers and the police.

In July 1877, Hayes sent federal troops to stop the fighting. Even though the workers lost, their strike led to the organization of unions. By the early 1900s, these unions would force companies to provide better job benefits and protection for their workers.

1

You will be drawing a type of train that was in use in the 1870s. To begin use a ruler to draw a long rectangle.

2

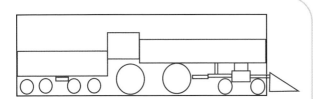

Use a ruler to draw three large rectangles to make the body of the train. Draw eight circles for the train's wheels. Add the smaller rectangles to make the engine parts of the train. Draw a triangle for the cowcatcher at the front.

3

Draw the outline of the top of the train using rectangles, curved lines, and straight lines. Add more to the bottom of the train using curved lines and small shapes. Add two vertical lines to the side of the train.

4

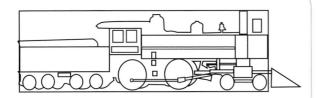

Draw the windows using rectangles. Draw the arm that connects the two large wheels. Add a long, thin rectangle to the body of the train. Add a rectangle between the two front wheels.

5

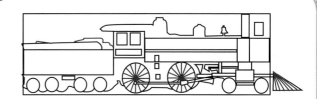

Draw the spokes of the large wheels and the slats of the cowcatcher using straight lines. Add curved and straight lines to the top of the train.

6

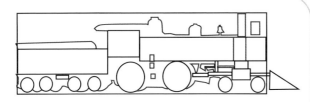

Draw the small details of the top and front using small circles, rectangles, and straight lines. Add details to the back of the train using straight lines.

7

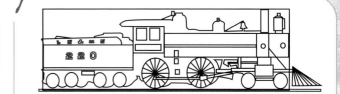

Print the letters "L S M S" on the rear of the train. Print the numbers "2 2 0" in the center of the rear of the train. Use a ruler to help draw the rail at the bottom of the train.

8

Erase the guide rectangle. Finish with detail and shading. Great job!

Hayes's Legacy

Hayes had promised during his campaign that he would not run for a second term of office. He kept that promise. When his presidency ended on March 4, 1881, he and Lucy retired to Spiegel Grove. Hayes continued to serve the nation by

speaking to various groups about the need for improvements in prisons and in education. He gave scholarships to needy African American students so that they could go to college, and he donated money to the Fremont, Ohio, library. On January 17, 1893, at age 70, Hayes had a heart attack and died. He is buried at Spiegel Grove.

During Hayes's four years as president, he tried to heal the bitter feelings between the North and the South by ending Reconstruction. Hayes entered the presidency after what was called one of the most dishonest elections in history. Once called the man who stole the presidency, Hayes is considered by historians today as an honest, but average, president.

1 You will be drawing Rutherford B. Hayes. Begin by drawing an oval for the head. This will be a guide that you will erase later. Draw lines for the neck and body. These will also be erased.

2 Draw guidelines across the front of the head oval. Draw lines around the body outline. This will become Hayes's neck and body. The guides will be erased later.

3 Erase the neck and body guides you drew in step 1. Draw the outline of Hayes's neck, shoulders, and left arm. Draw a triangle for the nose, almond shapes for the eyes, and an oval for the ear.

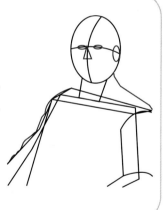

4 Erase the guidelines you added in steps 2. Draw the outline of the hair and beard. Draw the eyes and the nose.

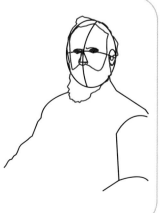

5 Erase the oval guide and the face and ear guides. Draw the vest on the front of his chest. Draw curved lines to show the folds of the sleeve on the right arm.

6 Draw the collars of the coat. Add another line to the vest. Erase the arm guidelines you added in step 2.

7 Draw a squiggly line and a curved line to show the mouth. Add button holes and buttons to the vest and the coat.

8 Finish with shading. The coat is dark and has a few heavy shadows in the folds. The shirt is white. The hair and the beard are shaded with squiggly lines. Great job!

Timeline

1822   Rutherford B. Hayes is born in Delaware, Ohio, on October 4.

1838–1842   Hayes attends Kenyon College.

1843–1845   Hayes attends Harvard Law School.

1845   Hayes moves to Fremont, Ohio, to practice law.

1847   Hayes meets Lucy Webb.

1850   Hayes moves to Cincinnati, Ohio.

1852   Hayes and Lucy marry.

1861   The Civil War begins.

Hayes joins the 23rd Regiment of Ohio Volunteers.

1862   Hayes is wounded in the Battle of South Mountain.

1865   The Civil War ends.

1865–1867   Hayes serves as a U.S. Representative.

1868–1872   Hayes serves as governor of Ohio.

1876   The Tilden-Hayes affair occurs.

1877   Hayes is chosen as president.

Hayes ends Reconstruction.

The Great Railroad Strike occurs. Hayes sends troops to stop the fighting.

1881   Hayes ends his one term as president and retires to Spiegel Grove.

1889   Lucy Hayes dies on June 25.

1893   Hayes dies on January 17.

Glossary

alcohol (AL-kuh-hol) A liquid, such as beer or wine, that can make a person lose control or get drunk.

amendment (uh-MEND-ment) An addition or a change to the Constitution.

architecture (AR-kih-tek-cher) The art of creating and making buildings.

civil rights (SIH-vul RYTS) The rights that citizens have.

compromise (KOM-pruh-myz) An agreement in which both sides give up something.

Constitution (kon-stih-TOO-shun) The basic rules by which the United States is governed.

designed (dih-ZYND) To have planned something.

donated (DOH-nayt-ed) To have given something away.

governor (GUH-vun-ur) An official elected as head of a state.

immigrants (IH-muh-grunts) People who move to a new country from another country.

inauguration (ih-naw-gyuh-RAY-shun) The event of swearing in a government official.

legacy (LEH-guh-see) Something that continues the memory of another person.

nominated (NAH-muh-nayt-ed) Suggested that someone or something should be given an award or a position.

quarry (KWOR-ee) An area of land where stones for building can be found.

Reconstruction (ree-kun-STRUK-shun) A period in U.S. history (1865–1877) after the Civil War, when the Confederate states attempted to rebuild.

reforms (rih-FORMZ) Changes or improvements.

regiment (REH-juh-ment) A group in the military.

reunion (ree-YOON-yun) A coming together of family, friends, or other groups of people.

scholarships (SKAH-ler-ships) Money given to people to pay for school.

seceded (sih-SEED-ed) To have withdrawn from a group or a country.

Union (YOON-yun) The Northern states that stayed with the federal government during the Civil War.

volunteers (vah-lun-TEERZ) Soldiers who choose to join the army.

Index

Web Sites

Due to the changing nature of Internet links, PowerKids Press has developed an online list of Web sites related to the subject of this book. This site is updated regularly. Please use this link to access the list:
www.powerkidslinks.com/kgdpusa/hayes/